To

You

For

You

With

Love

Catherine O'Connor

Grief
Is

AUSTIN MACAULEY PUBLISHERS™

LONDON • CAMBRIDGE • NEW YORK • SHARJAH

A CIP catalogue record for this title is available from the British Library.

ISBN 9781788233293 (Paperback)
ISBN 9781398434028 (ePub e-book)

www.austinmacauley.com

First Published (2021)
Austin Macauley Publishers Ltd
25 Canada Square
Canary Wharf
London
E14 5LQ

Is grief love?
Does grief love?
Does grief dance?
It is volatile
It is fickle
It picks
It chooses
It is different
It is indifferent
It is unique
To all humankind
Humankind
is
Unique

The
Silence
of
Grief
has
a
Deafening
Sound
Quiet
has
a
Still
Feeling
Loneliness
is
Immeasurable

No
No
No
No
No
No hope
Nowhere
Not now
Not
Ever

Day
by
Day
Find
Hope
Seek
Help
she
Said

Why?

Why not?

It is with me today

It is with others today

It will be with me tomorrow

It will be with others tomorrow

It will be with me everyday

It will be with others everyday

Face

It

Challenge

It

Question

It

There

Are

No

Answers

Grief
is
Universal
No
Dress
Code
No
Rules
Apply

Grief
Heightens
Humanity
Halts
People
Momentarily
a
Leveller
a
Time
to
Appreciate
to
Give
to
Value
Life
and
Love
to
Love

Grief
knows
No
Gender
has
No
Eyes
No
Ears
No
Mouth
No
Boundaries
It touches
It grips
It
is
Multi-cultural
It
Is
Multi-lingual

Grief
is
Greedy
Selfish
Spoiled
Wants
Everybody
Can't
Wait
No
Exceptions
No
Escape

Grief

is

Unpredictable

Impatient

It pounces

It creeps

It envelopes

It wraps

It lingers

It hops

It loiters

It labours

It drifts

It changes

It passes

S

L

O

W

L

Y

Grief
is
Part
of
Who
We
Are
Knocks
on
All
Doors
Each
Coping
Differently
Like the sore
On a finger
Your finger
My finger
It
T
H
R
O
B
S

Is that it?
Is it over?
She
Said
Nothing
Is that it?
Is it over?
Is he dead?
I'm afraid so
she
said
I
Said
N
O
T
H
I
N
G

Ravished by disease
Decaying cells
Holding on to life
Holding on to love
Holding on to us
Holding on to him
No glory in the end
Is that it?
Is it over?
She
Asks
Again

Ready for adventure
Full of life
Peak of the world
Ravished by the elements
Lost in China
Never to be found
No glory in the end
Is that it?
Is it over?
She
Asks
Again

Can't do

Can't move

Can't talk

Can't walk

Can't be

Can't understand

Can't touch

Can't feel

Can't see

Can't listen

Can't accept

Can't

Just

Can't

Just

Can't

Just

Can't

Want to talk about it

Shout

Scream

Tell the world

Warn the world

You tomorrow

Get ready

But

You

Will

Never

Be

Ready

Can't talk about it
Won't talk about it
No voice
No tongue
No
Sound
Can
I
Make
I
Am
Speechless
Hollow
Empty

Incongruent

Intangible

Inconsistent

Transient

Fickle

Ruthless

Fearless

Can't
Stay
Still
Change
Everything
Move
Everything
Don't
Think
Tomorrow
It could be me
Just do
Just be
Just move
through
the
fog
It
Lifts
It
Changes
Everyday

Emotions

Uncontrolled

Lash Out

Best Forgotten

Rest

Is

Impossible

It

Savages

It

Ravishes

It

Invades

It

is

R

E

L

E

N

T

L

E

S

S

First
It
is
a
Roller coaster
then
It
is
Blur
then
It
is
Pain
then
It
is
Everything
then
It
is
Nothing
then
It
Is
a
Waterfall
then
It
is
Still
then
there
are
Rocks
Pebbles
Sand
No
Anger
Just
Loss
Just
Missing
You
Missing
Us
Missing
Everything
Does acceptance come?

It is

It hurts

It will change

It will ease

It takes time

To let go

To unravel

Day

By day

Week

By week

Year

By

Year

Right brain
Left brain
Centre brain
Our brain
One brain
Two as one
Predicting
the
Unpredictable
Understanding
the
Unpredictable
the knowing glance
the shared smile
the shared laughter
the shared moments
Nobody else
can
Understand
or
will
Understand

Grief

Grabs

Grief

Holds

Grief

Changes

Us

Temporarily

Permanently

Unusual

Emotions

Volatile

Ordinary

Yet

Unsolvable

Challenges

Insurmountable

In

Desperation

I

Cry

Out

But

Nobody

Hears

My new friend

a

Little

Anaesthesia

to

block out the sounds

the bowl in the sink with the stagnant water

the fly buzzing a little

Stopping and buzzing again

the bed unmade

the kettle cold

the post unopened in the hall

the garden unattended

the windows

Closed

the doors

Closed

I
Stopped
By the door
and looked
Was I that desperate?
Was I the addict?
The outcast or the homeless?
Or just lost without soul?
the brass bell rang
the door opened
I announced myself
was at once received
No words said
I felt safe
From the noise
of
Grief
a
First
Step

2 chairs

1 table

1 box of tissues

1 glass of water

2 people

1 leading

1 feeding

Talking softly

It

Helps

a

Little

Each

Time

It
is
Tiresome
Wearisome
Troublesome
Sad
Sorrowful
Painful
It
Takes
Many
Forms
Shapes
Sizes
It
Envelopes
by surprise
It pounces
It
H
O
V
E
R
S

Some days
Make no sense
No morning
No evening
No sunrise
No sunset
No light
No darkness
Just time
Unaccounted time
Time wanted
Time wasted
Time spent
in
a
Vacuum
Emotionless
Loveless
Powerless
It
Will
Change
It
Will
Pass

Lines
Appear
where
No
Lines
Were
Before
Eyes
Gloss
Over
I
Can't
See
I
Look
in
the
Mirror
but
there
is
Nobody
there

Creases

Everywhere

My

Face

My

Head

My brow

My

Brain

My

Body

My

Hands

My

Feet

Sorrow

Fills

the

Crevices

Is

This

Me?

I
Don't
Cry
I
Can't
Cry
I
Want
to
Cry
but
maybe
I
have
Cried
Already
Are tears only
in our eyes
or
Are they in our hearts
Our lungs, our minds,
Our souls, our limbs
Our blood?
We can't always reach them

They
Do
Not
Know
What
to
Do
or
Say
so
They
Say
Nothing
They
Don't
Ask
It
Hurts
I
Understand
Reluctantly

Sorry for your loss
Sorry for your troubles
You were lucky
You are lucky
Am I lucky?
Bereft
of
My love
My life
My fire
My soul
My body
My brain
Don't
A
S
K

Ask

Me

How

I

Am

I

Answer

High-pitched

Doing

Well

Doing fine

Fine

Fine

Fine

Fine

F

I

N

E

Blue, purple, navy,
Red, green
All
Colours
for
All
Occasions
Documents
for
Identification
Apparel
Hangs
Still
Undisturbed
Time
to
Disturb
Must
Disturb
the
Clock
Strikes
Twelve

A
Large
Bin
Hungers
to
Greet
to
Clear
the
Clutter
to
Make
Noise
to
Disturb
to
Bring
Order
the
Clock
Strikes
Twelve
Again

Order

Meets

Disorder

Order

Wins

Light

Prevails

Spring

Comes

Garden

Tended

Blooms

Appear

Roses

Pruned

As if with anger

the

Secateurs

Ravishing the stems

Weeds

Choking

Your

Daffodils

Survival
is
Key
to
Life
Life
is
Survival
Give
Life
Permission

I wonder
Why six feet under
Why not ten or
Twenty or two
or four?
What's down there?
Is it cold I wonder?
No
Blanket
to
Comfort
No
Sun
to
Warm
No
Songs
to
Sing
Stone
is
Cold

The grey stone marks
your existence
Neatly
A bare patch
Remains
Unattended
Maybe I'll leave
it that way
so you can breathe
a little
and wait
for
the
Next
Dig
when my existence
will be marked
Neatly
Beneath
Yours

I
Stop
Today
as
a
Wave
Breathes
Over
me
Unexpectedly
I
Wonder
Why?
Was it a dream?
Was it a familiar smell?
Was it the sorrow of others?
That brought me back
Temporarily
I hope
Temporarily
I
Hope
Temporarily
I
Hope

Be kind
for
Kindness
is
Gentle
Soothing
Enabling
Empowering
Comforting
Affirming
Confirming
Softening
In
Grief
I
Hunger
for
Kindness

Light
Peeps
through
my
Darkness
Hope
follows
Softness
follows
a
Glint
of
Happiness
That's allowed
for
Recovery
to
Reluctantly
Try
to
Move
On

I
Feel
a
Faint
Breeze
of
Calm
a
Butterfly
Flits
and
Flutters
in
my
Path
No
Sound
Just
Beauty
Y
O
U

Beautiful

Morning

Breathing

Through

My

Pores

Silence

Lifting

Loneliness

Tolerable

There is hope

There is life

There is love

There is a future

Repeat out loud

a

Future

a

Future

a

Future

I
Feel
Happy
Today
in
Good
Company
Having
Fun
It's ok to be happy
It's delightful
after
All the pain and sorrow
It
is
Uplifting
Hold
On
T
I
G
H
T

Reflect

Smile

Laugh

Love

Like

You

Used

To

If

You

Can

The
Sun
is
Beautiful
Shining
Through
Negotiating
its share
Barriers within
Acknowledge
Shut out
the pain
Turning to the light
It's good
to
Feel
Good
Again

If only for one day
What would we do?
Where would we go?
Would we chat awhile?
and laugh together
Break bread at table
with ours
or
Visit far flung places
of
Ancient cities
or
Walk the beach
Our beach
I walk that beach
for you
and think
If only for one day
But then
The clock would
Tick loudly and the
Day would end
Death is a once off
Memories are forever

Lines

Begin

to

Smooth

a

Freshness

Appears

I

Look

in

the

Mirror

I

Do

Not

Recognise

Her

The doors

are open

The windows

are open

The garden

is tended

The kettle

is warm

The bed

is made

Is yours

a

Tea

or

a

Coffee?

Come, Come

Sit in the sun

Isn't

the

Light

Beautiful

Thank you
for gifts
of kindness
of thought
of spirit
of encouragement
of nourishment
of help with all things
to
Pick
me
Up
to
Keep
my
Heart
Alive
I
Will
Falter
Momentarily
I
Hope
Momentarily
I hope
but you will be there

And in time
I will
be there
for
You

Catherine O'Connor, Education Consultant and Author, draws on life's experience unravelling the journey of grief in poetic form.

This book is for anyone, young or old, who has lost a loved one.

Reflective and profound.

She lives in Dublin, Ireland.

CPSIA information can be obtained
at www.ICGtesting.com
Printed in the USA
LVHW021032050821
694613LV00010B/797